Anonymous

Fraud and Fair dealing in Stocks!

An Exposé of the Impositions practiced, especially on Country and distant Dealers, through the U. S. Mails and otherwise

Anonymous

Fraud and Fair dealing in Stocks!
An Exposé of the Impositions practiced, especially on Country and distant Dealers, through the U. S. Mails and otherwise

ISBN/EAN: 9783337216412

Printed in Europe, USA, Canada, Australia, Japan

Cover: Foto ©Suzi / pixelio.de

More available books at **www.hansebooks.com**

FRAUD
AND
FAIR DEALING
IN
STOCKS!

AN EXPOSÉ
Of the Impositions Practiced, especially on Country and Distant Dealers, through the U. S. Mails and otherwise.

BY A NEW YORK STOCK BROKER.

New York:
JOHN THOMPSON, Jr.
52 Broadway.
1880.

Copyright Secured.

FRAUD
AND
FAIR DEALING
IN
STOCKS!

AN EXPOSÉ

Of the Impositions Practiced, especially on Country and Distant Dealers, through the U. S. Mails and otherwise.

BY A NEW YORK STOCK BROKER.

New York:
JOHN THOMPSON, Jr.
52 Broadway.
1880.

FRAUD AND FAIR DEALING IN STOCKS.

I.

A Little Story of the Past.

Something more than a year since, conducting the business of stock-brokerage in a reputable and what we intended to be in a beneficial manner, and aware how easily many persons in the same line of business managed to make it tricky and disreputable, we necessarily were somewhat anxious to discover and expose any false and unreliable members of the guild. Acting at that time for the benefit of all who were interested in stocks, or who intended to be so, we necessarily watched closely any publications claiming to be of the same character, and yet bearing the evidences of those tricks and false representations which have done so much, during the last dozen years, to discredit an honest profession, and reduce it, in many minds, to the level of the very lowest gambling. It was entirely in such interests that we proposed to deal, with ungloved hands, with those who gave evidence of prostituting the business of stock-dealing to something very like the "confidence" of the police courts, as it is in the same interests that we now pursue the subject at greater length.

For some months before that time there had appeared, with the ostensible publication office of "— Exchange Place," and an imprint at the foot of the last column, stamping it as the issue of "Dorrance & Co., Bankers and Brokers, — & — Broad St. and — & — Exchange Place, New York City," a publication of four pages, modeled something after the outward appearance of ordinary small trade-journals, and bearing the name of *The New York Stock Announcer*. A little more closely examined, by any one familiar with the "tricks of the trade," it was seen to be printed on the back or blank side of the circular issued monthly by *The Daily Indicator*, giving the stock quotations for the month; but that the whole thing had been laboriously prepared by and for *The New York Stock Announcer*, was shown by the fact that the name of that journal was printed at the head of each table-page. With this last proof added, what distant client or intending stock-dealer could doubt that "Dorrance & Co." had taken the pains to complete a table especially for him and others like him, and that they stood among the reputable stock-brokers of New York? Perhaps there might have been even less difficulty in so accrediting "Dorrance & Co." from the fact that, whatever the actual constituency of the firm, the name had been well chosen, as the name of Dorrance was usually more than respectable, and a well-known banking house of the City had for years borne a name sounding enough like the one in question, to make mistake easy and deception convenient.

With this single fact we might have had the right to claim a "broiling" as the due of the "Dorrances," for reputable firms are naturally very careful to do nothing ambiguous, and the mint-mark of unreliability is almost always attempted deception and sailing under colors really belonging to others.

But all this was, meanwhile, a mere trifle in the necessary exposure. A second publication, and one of much more consequence, emanated from this remarkable firm, bearing the copyright notice of "Dorrance & Co.," and the same imprint which we have already noted as at the foot of the last column of *The New York Stock Announcer.* This, of eight pages, and printed on blue paper (probably from some allusion to the old phase of compliment, "true blue"), was in some regards one of the most remarkable productions of the century. *Imprimis*, it bore on the first page, a very handsomely engraved picture of a noble building, of five stories besides the basement and mansard, with two porticos, towered mansard façade, a five-story wing on the one side, with not less than a dozen rows of windows, and on the other a Grecian building which might be the Parthenon at Athens and might be the United States Sub-Treasury. Over the wing of this noble structure floated the American flag—presumably the especial emblem of the high-toned and patriotic "Dorrance & Co."; and on the end of the main building, in letters indicating at least two feet display in actual size, reads the honored legend, "Dorrance & Co., Bankers and Brokers." No better evidence could be needed that "Dorrance & Co." were the presiding geniuses of all this range of buildings, and that whoever else might occupy any part of them, those persons unknown amounted to little or nothing. For who else than the all-prevailing firm of "Dorrance & Co." could have a right to cover the whole end of the building with a sign in that manner, and after the mode which some of us have seen adopted at Paris, where a large firm of haberdashers or dealers in silks and velvets buys the privilege of daubing over the whole end of his palace, of the impecunious Duke of Thingamy or Count Whatshisname? And what mere ordinary mortal dared hazard the assertion, that all this picture and the sign on the end, and " — & — Broad Street and — & — Exchange Place" below it, were nothing more nor less than a mere and shameless "plant" for gudgeons?—"Dorrance & Co." occupying one or two small rooms at the end of the wing, up one or more flights of stairs, and the building thus quietly appropriated being one of the noblest financial structures in America, at the corner of two of New York's most noted commercial streets, with the occupancy of which the said "Dorrance & Co." had just as much to do as with that of the Tower of London!

Something, now, of the verbal contents of this publication so illustriously illustrated.

In the opening of this document, perhaps the system of "Socratian reasoning" was about as deftly carried out as one could find it in a long day. It traveled by "steps," after that system, and without any faltering. (1.) To make money was the laudable desire of every man. (2.) Wall Street, with Broad Street and Exchange Place superadded, was the place to make it. (3.) Stock-brokers were necessary. (4.) Some of these might be reliable and some the reverse, but for the clean thing it was indispensable to go to "Dorrance & Co." (5.) "Dorrance & Co." did well by all, and in all modes; but by the "combination plan of operating in stocks," they made millionaires universally as inevitably.

(6.) There was an injunction to join this combination, send on your money, leave it in the hands of "Dorrance & Co.," and don't ask too many questions—and—there you are! When to this were added the "History of Jay Gould's Fortune," the "Unerring Rules for Success," the reasons "Why Combinations Pay Large Profits," and the offer to transact business miscellaneously on *one per cent. margin*, it may be said that the man who could not see a fortune in dealing with "Dorrance & Co." must have been either blind or—the reverse.

See how magnificently "Dorrance & Co." realized this promise, dealing with one of their customers, who afterwards had the magnanimity to place the documents in our hands, especially that the noble firm might be honored as they deserved. This client, say John Jones, of Hardscrabble, Illinois, had forwarded a certain amount to the operators; and imagine the joy of the aforesaid John Jones, of Hardscrabble, on receiving the subjoined document (also on blue paper):

OFFICE OF DORRANCE & COMPANY,
NEW YORK, Dec. 13, 1878.

DEAR SIR: We take pleasure in informing you that we made a turn on Northwestern, selling short $47\frac{1}{4}$ and covering at $46\frac{3}{4}$, realizing a profit of $\frac{1}{2}$ per cent., being equivalent to $50.00 profit on each 100 shares of stock.

Yours respectfully,

DORRANCE & COMPANY.

N. B.—Profits and original capital to be used as working capital until the close.

The joy of John Jones, it is true, might have been a trifle damped at the concluding announcement: "Profits and original capital to be used as working capital until the close." "Close" of what? The firm's solvency? The man's life? The century? The duration of the world? This was a trifle ambiguous; and Jones would possibly have preferred to have the $50.00 forwarded to him, even in trade dollars at freight charges. But he was a patient man, and he waited—confident in the high standing of "Dorrance & Co.," and hoping for the best. Waited until the reception of document No. 2 (also on blue paper—perhaps this time indicative of the state of mind of the—we had almost said "victim," but prefer to say "out-of-town stock-dealer"):

OFFICE OF DORRANCE & CO..
NEW YORK, Dec. 20th, 1878.

DEAR SIR: We regret to inform you that we made a very unlucky turn with the combination in which you were interested, selling Northwestern short at 47, after which the stock advanced so rapidly, that the entire capital of this combination, together with the profits that we had already made, notice of which we had previously sent you, were entirely lost.

We regret exceedingly that this move was unsuccessful.

However, if you will take another venture and send us another remittance, we will do all in our power to make it a success and retrieve this loss, thereby retaining your patronage in the future, as we have many others.   Yours respectfully,

DORRANCE & CO.

Whether, on receipt of this second document, the "out-of-town stock-dealer" went and blew out his brains, does not appear in this connection; but it does appear that if he had any of those brains remaining, and concluded still to live on the habitable earth, he put all the possible degrees of longitude between himself and "Dorrance & Co.," unless he had occasion to make one more transient investment, in harness leather, and use it on the backs of dealers who felt so little shame in making away with his money, and who displayed so much cheek in asking for more of it to be made away with in the same manner!

II.

SOME THINGS THAT HAVE SINCE HAPPENED.

All this healthy little exposé, made by us in the interest of fair dealing and public good, took place something more than a year ago. We should not like to be brought on the stand to make oath that that exposé, boldly written and having a wide circulation over the United States, did not do something to awake the attention of government authorities to the game that was being so extensively played, and to the necessity of some measures being taken to check the evil, if the financial community was not to be literally honey-combed. At all events, the attention of the authorities *was* called to the abuse; and the authorities, under the right given them by the necessary use of the United States Mails for carrying on the details of all those operations, went to work at the cleansing of this new "Augean stable." For months past they have been pursuing that work, with somewhat more energy than the other branches of the government have shown in the Indian question —yes, almost as much as still another has shown in pulling apart the packages landed from steamships and discovering whether Mr. William Smith has not one more coat, or Mrs. Susan Thompson (with a *p*) one more silk dress, than the revenue laws of the United States allow to be imported by one person.

That they did not set to work any too soon is very evident from what has preceded. That they could not perform any more meritorious duty than to tie the hands of the unscrupulous and thus protect the public, is equally evident.

The devices of financial tricksters are many, and perhaps no field offers such remunerative results as through the United States Mail. The majority of American people are curious, and their curiosity has often been the cause of the loss of many a hard-earned dollar, as many out of mere curiosity have replied to a seductive advertisement of fabulous gains from minute investments, often forwarding small sums by way of experiment, which, in most cases, resulted in small profits, and an enticing communication asking for a larger remittance. Then, the confidence having been easily bought, the victim before long finds himself the loser to a heavy extent. Others pressed for money send what they have, in the hope of securing more to meet the demands made upon them; others from greed of gain. It would perhaps be impossible to enumerate the causes that induce the unsuspecting to entrust their money to firms and individuals of whom they know nothing beyond their own representations.

The quickness with which money had been made and lost in Wall Street offered an exceptional field for the sharpers, through the various modes of stock operations, and glittering comparisons of what might have been done, when placed in skillfully-worded circulars. Books and papers made easy prey of the country dealers; while the result of the swindle has been passed by, by the majority, in their desire to cover from their friends and employers the fact that they were "gambling in stocks." Thus the swindle continues, with "fresh fish" indefinitely, the very opportunities for being warned thus going out of the chances.

The profitableness of these schemes attracted others of the same class, till the various stock concerns attained such numbers that complaints continued to pour into the Post Office and Exchanges to such an extent that the Postal authorities and the New York Stock Exchange were compelled to make effort to break up the business of these fraudulent dealers who transacted business through the mails. In November, 1878, the Law Committee of the Stock Exchange formally authorized a special agent in whom they had full confidence, "to collect all the information possible concerning the firms that were using the mails and the press to defraud the public by means of bogus transactions in stocks, and use all legal means to secure the conviction of the offending parties."

This agent at once advertised for communications from parties who were dissatisfied with their dealings with the magnificent "Dorrance & Co.," one of the firms in question, and from them obtained much evidence in the shape of the correspondence of that firm. When that portion of the case had been sufficiently covered, the services of another gentleman were obtained for the further prosecution of the matter, and his knowledge and experience of this class of fraud through the mails soon enabled him to obtain such additional evidence as resulted in the complete overthrow of the fraudulent system. An order was issued by the Postmaster-General, forbidding the delivery of letters and money-orders to about a score of different concerns, the order being based upon the evidence submitted to the Department. Of course this closed the obnoxious concerns, at a blow,—while it is only fair to say that discredit was meanwhile thrown upon other and reputable firms, not at all engaged in the swindling operations, but who, suffering from the association, have been seriously damaged and many of them ruined or obliged to close business no longer profitable.

III.

Why This Exposé.

It is a matter of question whether any man has any more right to conceal a knowledge which he holds, calculated to save the community from injury if scattered abroad, than he has to disseminate false statements to work the injury for his own advantage. That we so held, more than a year ago, we have already shown; and while not at all agreeing with the government authorities in estimation of some of the processes used by them in carrying out the object of repression, we have held, and do hold, to our old bebelief of individual duty. Without having laid ourselves liable to the charge of double-dealing in any manner or form, we have been engaged, as already said, in stock-broking, and have consequently been placed entirely "behind the curtain" in watching the operations of others who have placed themselves at once under the ban of the law and of the morals of finance. With this information at hand, we undoubtedly have it in our power to save the community uncounted thousands of dollars, if they pay heed to the warnings and explanations which we offer them. Not a word here set down, but is written in the best interests of humanity; and not a word, so far as we know or believe, but has behind it the guaranty of entire truth and fair dealing to all.

IV.

WHAT ARE LEGITIMATE STOCK OPERATIONS?

In order to understand more easily what are the illegitimate stock operations, into which the raft of speculators of whom "Dorrance & Co." and their compeers have led so many thousands of the American public and filched from them so many hundreds of thousands (probably millions!) of dollars, it may be necessary to say a few words as to what constitutes legitimate stock operations. To that duty, then, and to the position held by bona-fide dealers in stocks, before proceeding with the other branch of the subject.

What are "stocks" most men know, even those most remote from the business centres of this and other countries. Great enterprises, requiring large amounts of money to inaugurate them and to carry them on, require the funds of many people to be thrown together in order to make up the necessary amounts. In order to make this practicable, those great enterprises are set on foot with a declaration of the amount of money which is to be represented in any one of them; and in order to make the handling of those amounts in an intelligent way possible, the whole sum represented in any one enterprise is divided up into so many "shares" of the whole, at so much per share. The "Through-To-China Mining Company," say, or the "Shinglesburg and Woodstown Railway Company," or the "Highflyer National Banking Company," is organized, with a requirement of Two Millions capital. That will be divided, say again, into 20,000 shares, at $100 each. So represented, those stocks are in shape to be handled—in other words, made a marketable commodity; and they go upon the stock market, accordingly, precisely as so many barrels of flour or bales of shirtings go upon the market appropriate to *them.*

Then it follows, very naturally, that the price of shares in any given enterprise does not continue at the same figure, and that while one man wishes to realize on any shares that he may hold, go out, and put his money into his pocket or into some other business, another man wishes to buy in. Many wishing to go out, at any one time, with few wishing to invest in that direction, must make a decline, and vice versa. Or, the "Through-To-China" strikes metal more precious than the original owners had supposed, and the worth of it, or of its shares, necessarily rises in proportion. Or, the "Shinglesburg and Woodstown Railway," after being fairly established, finds the bulk of its traffic taken away by the "Shoal River Steamboat Line," and the worth of its shares decline accordingly. Or, one of the large stockholders in either is driven to the wall, and needs to realize on his investment, with some suddenness, and he cannot expect to find full price in the brief period allowed him. Or, a new millionaire comes into the field, with strong desires after stocks of almost any sort, and he "boosts" the whole list by lavish buying. Nothing more than this is necessary as showing the fact that "stocks" are not only a marketable commodity, but that they are and must necessarily be fluctuating, to some extent, in their values.

V.

WHO ARE LEGITIMATE STOCK DEALERS?

It goes without saying that, of everything demanded, there will be found a supply. The exceptions to this rule are so infrequent (except where a poor fellow chances to want a dinner and cannot find it, or a creditor demands his bill and is told to "call again") that the adage may be set down as a universal one. Every community requires sheetings, broadcloths, flannels, flour, and potatoes; and every community finds an early supply of dealers in those commodities. Precisely so with stocks, the trading in which, either as principal or broker, may be called quite as legitimate as that in dry goods or groceries, and only a small proportion more risky. Stock-dealers (that is, men dealing in stocks on their own account, and making or losing money by the rise or fall of the commodity in hand) are supplemented by stock-brokers (that is, men who act as agents for the purchase and sale of stocks for others); and very often, and indeed generally, the two avocations become one

No ordinary citizen can hope to keep so well acquainted with the fluctuations of the stock market as a man who deals in that commodity day by day, and necessarily watches all the quotations and keeps account of all the important transactions. Consequently, literally the whole business of the purchase and sale of stocks passes into the hands of stockbrokers—acting for their own account or for their customers. And in no calling of the age is the very highest honor considered to be more absolutely necessary than in that under consideration—both sides to the contract involved. The dealer who will leave his broker in the lurch, is considered several degrees meaner than the ordinary defaulter; and the broker who will deceive and swindle his principal, is considered—well, scarcely the person to hold a seat in the Stock Board much longer than the time necessary to legally expel him. A very high standard of reliability is necessary, on both sides; alas, that it is not always found, even with firms who run their signs along the whole side of a building belonging to some one else!

VI.

How Stocks are Legitimately Bought and Sold.

Suppose that Mr. William Wilkins desires to possess himself, either as a mere investment for money on hand, or because he believes that it will be directly worth more than at present, of $50,000 worth of stock of the "Shinglesburg & Woodstown Railroad." He can, of course, buy for himself; but he is not likely, unless with some connection in that line, to do so. He goes to a broker, orders the purchase of 500 shares (the par value $100 each), and deposits his check for $10,000 as

"MARGIN,"

to make the broker safe in the event of his failing to call and take it up as promised. From that $10,000 the broker, in case of the customer's default, has the means and the right to take his percentage-fee, and to reimburse himself in the event of his being obliged to sell the purchased stock at a loss. All things working smoothly, it is to be presumed that the stock becomes the property of Mr. William Wilkins. Then, later, Mr. Wilkins may wish to sell the same stock. He puts it into the hands of the broker (who may or may not make him an advance on it), with instructions to hold it for a certain price, or to sell within a certain time, whatever may be the figure attainable. The broker sells, deducts what he has already paid (if anything), takes out his percentage, and returns the balance to Mr. Wilkins. This is the whole story of the legitimate buying and selling of stocks, and of the connection held with it by the broker who merely acts as an agent in the transaction. Of course there is something very different in the case of the broker himself being the owner of the stocks at the time when Mr. Wilkins wishes to make the purchase, or in the other case of his being personally the buyer of them from Mr. Wilkins.

In this has been shown what may be called the "hard-pan" of stock dealing—the operation with a money basis sufficient to make it safe. But, as every one can easily understand, out of it grows something quite different—at first only a little so, but in the extreme so far removed from the status of this transaction that it would scarcely be recognized by the nearest relative as the same. *Speculation* comes in—speculation, more or less reckless, but in its nature always no little risky. Men wish to deal in stocks who have very little money to employ, who believe that they see a "big thing" in some certain operation, but to whom a failure in that operation means complete ruin, or, if that is already accomplished, something worse. They carry out the story of the greedy boy who attempted to take his hand from the jar while it was too full; and they very often meet with a corresponding fate. They seek to manage enterprises altogether beyond them—to "bear" stocks (*i. e.*, run down their price) so that they can buy what they wish or need at their own prices, or to "bull" them (*i. e.*, drive up the prices so that they may be able to sell what they want to dispose of at profitable figures); and in either of those operations, if not well backed by the efforts of others working to the same end, they are very apt to come to grief. And when they do so, the next thing to be heard is a wail over the iniquity of the stock-broker, who may have had, really, nothing more to do with the arrangement than one of the wheels, itself pulled along, has in propelling a wagon. Not that all stock-brokers, with seats in the Board and every reason to keep up their reputations, are always honest and high-minded. By no means. The Black Fridays, and other notable days of the New York Stock Market, show only too well that there may be rottenness even in the high places of trade. But even with such of them as have an ambiguous record in some particulars we have nothing to do in the present instance; our aim is to expose other and very different persons, for the benefit of those who have the disadvantage of distance, and who could not be warned without some such explanation as that which we are making.

VII.

WHERE THIS SPECIAL VILLAINY COMES IN.

We have shown, in our very brief explanation of fair stock dealing, that purchases of stocks are very often made, and ordered to be made, without the paying down, by the person ordering, of any such amount of money as would cover the purchase. We have explained that "margins" are very often depended upon—that is, certain proportions of the amounts of the purchases, to be used by the broker as his protection, and, very often, as a part of the means through which he makes the desired purchases. It is very evident, to the slowest comprehension, that the system is a temptation—that many a man, who would not dream of being able to purchase a block of stock in any special mining, railroad or other company that he might happen to desire, if he was required to pay down the whole amount of cash for the purchase, is likely to take the risk of paying down *a part*, if the balance can be carried for him, with the hope that the speculation may turn out what he has believed, and that, consequently, he can make money out of the capital of others. It does not need twice looking to know that the speculator very soon finds brokers who will accommodate him, and indeed assist him, in any imprudence which he may be disposed to commit; and it is also obvious that after a time this speculator, if he is a "greenhorn" (as is very probable), will find some broker more or less disreputable, who will take his "margin," pretend to use it honestly, and yet so manipulate the special stock as to make the speculator a loser while he himself pockets a very neat profit.

VIII.

How This Manipulation Can Be Done.

" How can the broker, even if dishonest enough, so manipulate a stock as to be himself a winner while his customer is a loser, when the two are, through the 'margin' and the purchase for mutual interest, something very like partners ?" Such is the question very often asked, and the question very certain to be asked at this stage of our exposé. And no one in the world can be more easily answered ! The purchaser has put into the hands of the broker a certain amount of money, *on the supposition that the broker knows more about the thing to be dealt in than himself.* So he does, unquestionably ; and if he is a dishonest man, he knows more about it than his customer will *ever* know ! As thus :

Suppose that Peter Smith, a would-be speculator, has placed in the hands of his broker, Timothy Sharp, $20,000 as margin, with orders to buy him a block of one thousand shares in the Squeedonck and Hardscrabble Railway, par value one hundred dollars per share, and range of late sales very nearly at par, —telling Sharp to secure the stock at the best terms that he can within a week, when he will be back to town. He goes away to St. Louis or to Montreal. Within three days after he is gone, Squeedonck and Hardscrabble runs down from 98 to 92. Sharp, watching the market, buys at once. Two days afterwards, it "booms" again—say to 96½. Sharp quietly makes the entry on his books, of one thousand shares, bought for Peter Smith, at 96½. He then holds the stock. Smith, a little unfortunate in the turn of his affairs at Montreal or St. Louis, comes back to town at the appointed time—the end of one week. He finds Squeedonck and Hardscrabble a trifle down again, say at 94. A little disappointed, but needing money more than he had anticipated, he orders Sharp to sell. Sharp does so. Now let us see how the bank books of the two gentlemen will stand, without reckoning the small commissions to which Sharp is entitled, twice, both as buyer and seller. Smith is charged with $96,500, and credited with $94,000; deficit, besides the commission, $2,500. Sharp has paid out $92,000, and received $96,500; gain, $4,500, besides the commissions. If Sharp is at all the keen villain that we take him to be, he has so covered his tracks that no one knows that he purchased at 92 instead of $96\frac{1}{2}$; if Smith is not a keener man than the majority of his brothers, he may swear a little, and among other things swear that he will never deal in stocks again—never, no more!—but he will never be able to get beyond the merest suspicion as to what bit him, even if he reaches that suspicion at all.

It may happen that Squeedonck and Hardscrabble, after its fluctuations, has, before the time of Smith's return to town, taken another turn, and gone up to par, where Smith certainly expected that it would be by that time, when ordering the purchase. In that case, Smith will be the gainer by some $3,500, less the commissions; but Sharp will, none the less, be his $4,500 ahead, unless, in the prospect of Smith's making too much, he concludes to charge him with the purchase as made at 97½ instead of 96¼, thus pocketing $1,000 more ($5,500, besides commissions) and reducing Smith's gains to $2,500, less commissions. In one word, Sharp has the whole thing in his hands, and Smith (mind, that we are only speaking of *greenhorn* Smith, not Smith the expert!) is exactly wax in his hands, to be manipulated at will for a time, even if not for a very long one.

IX.

"DISTANCE LENDS ENCHANTMENT, ETC."

Here comes in the point making this exposé so specially valuable, if those for whom it is designed will pay close attention to it. Had Smith stayed in town and watched the stock market closely, even with a broker to do his buying for him, and had Sharp been aware that Smith was in town and so watching, the story would have been very different in some of the details. *Scoundrelly stock-brokers make most of their money out of persons residing at a distance from the City, simply because they do so reside and are thus* NOT IN THEIR WAY.

The foregoing has made it reasonably plain that the farther away from the City and the chances of hourly intelligence the customer may be, the better will be found the opportunity to deal with him in a money-making manner—to put the fact in that mild form. So much being understood, and the fact added that the intention of the dishonest broker is to engage the attention more particularly of the more ignorant, who do not even keep themselves posted to the degree that the newspapers might make possible for them, let us see

X.

How Country Customers Are Made and Served.

We have already said, in the exposé (or if we have not we should have done so), that Americans are a credulous people and a speculative one. This applies particularly to those who reside outside of the sound of any of the City bells, and who, indeed, only know the great cities by occasional visits or by the communications received and sent through the mails. For some cause, not necessary to explain, when a man, however "green" originally, has removed to one of those great cities, and resided for a considerable time within the range of its influences, he "dries" very materially. In other words, he becomes more suspicious of his neighbors than he was in the days when he dwelt among green fields and felt the free air of heaven instead of the smoky atmosphere of a city on his cheek. He is not so good a man, probably, because not so frank and trusting as he was of old. It is doubtful whether he would do as many generous things, when the opportunity for them was brought under his notice, as he would have done when residing in the country; and it is just possible that he is less shocked at the developments of vice in the aggregate than he might once have been. But he is a *safer* man, after long residence in the City, than he was when he first came, or before removal to it. Safer, as against the assaults and tricks of others, whatever he may be as against the assaults of the Great Enemy, who "goes about seeking whom he may devour."

Let it be understood, then, that the average man of the country is "green," as against thousands of tricks which might be detected in a moment by the City man. But he has something even worse and more dangerous than his "greenness." While quite willing to adopt for himself and his the praise of being better than the City residents, he is *not* willing. to hear the accusation of being "behind the times" in anything. He is entirely unwilling to acknowledge that there is anything which the City men knows, hidden from him. He keeps up his interest in the City by newspapers and other communications. He partially feels that he belongs to the City and that the City belongs to him. Let him understand that there is something connected with the *mysteries* of the metropolis, in which he may hope to have a hand without expatriating himself from his fields or his country-village workshop, and he is very happy indeed. When arrived at this stage of thinking, as he is very likely to be at an early day, after having placed himself, even temporarily, beyond absolute need, he is exactly in the mood to receive any poison that the stock-broker or other scoundrel may choose to disseminate. Send him a circular, *sealed* (it is always best to have it sealed, as it excites double confidence), and he literally gloats over being the possessor of certain knowledge not shared by those around him. He is, then, at about the ripe and proper period for being "let in," and the unscrupulous broker lets him in accordingly.

XI.

WHAT IS TO BE DONE.

What is to be done by the said unscrupulous broker is, in a word, to get a certain amount of money out of the country victim, amuse him as long as it is possible to bleed him any more, and take good care that, whenever the connection may close, *he (the victim) never sees a penny of the money back, unless in the shape of bait for himself or others, with larger amounts to be hauled in.*

XII.

THE MACHINERY USED.

The machinery by which the swindling operations of rogueish brokers as against outsiders is carried on, may be grouped together in a very few words. The names are most of them a trifle slangy, but that is of no consequence, especially to the man who has been nipped in any one of them. They consist of "Puts," "Calls," "Spreads," "Straddles," with the already explained "Margins" working in connection. The man who buys a "Put," buys in it the privilege of making the seller of it take a certain amount of stock, at a given price, within a certain length of time. The man who buys a "Call," buys in it the privilege of requiring the seller to deliver a certain amount of stock, at a given price, within a certain length of time. The purchaser of a "Straddle" obtains in it the right to elect, within a certain time, whether he will buy or sell a certain stock at a certain figure; and the buyer of a "Spread" has nearly the same, excepting that the "Spread" combines a "Put" and "Call" at a certain percentage *from* the market, instead of being *at* the market as is the case with a "Straddle." "Margin," as already explained, is the amount put up by any purchaser, to make the dealer supposedly safe in perfecting the transaction in behalf of the customer. With these explanations we may be able to point out, somewhat intelligently,

XIII.

How The Customer Is Gone For.

Specious pamphlets and yet more specious circulars are sent out broadcast over the land. And yet scarcely "broadcast," for seed sown in that way falls upon the land anywhere, without any intelligent direction, and such is not the case in the sending out of pamphlets and circulars. *Lists* are the thing in demand; lists, of the people who have money or property, in one State or another, and who (the whole truth must be told!) are supposed to be silly enough to be likely to fall into the traps of illegitimate speculation. How are these lists obtained? How should *we* know? They are obtained, perhaps, in something like the same way in which the Mercantile Agencies arrive at the knowledge of the commercial standing of the residents of the whole land, from Maine to the Florida Capes. Of course some of these lists are blunders, or worse, and those who depend upon them simply waste their time and money (as, by the way, most of those do who depend upon the information supplied by the Mercantile Agencies; but that is "neither here nor there"). In some way, the lists are obtained. The poll-lists made for town meetings and elections, the tax-lists, the rolls of lodges, even some of the rolls of membership of the churches, are said to supply information to those so greedy for it.

The rest of the names (and indeed a large part of them) are obtained by advertising "Wonderful Chances to Make Money," and a few other things of the sort, in the daily and weekly papers, and making use, for further sending, of the names that are appended to the inquiries with reference to how the writers can avail themselves of those great privileges and opportunities. These "first bites" may be said to be legion; and they give very good hope to the operator of "more to follow."

The names once obtained, as already said, out go the pamphlets and circulars by the hundred thousand. Men living in Peoria, Podunk, and indeed all over the Union, who had no idea whatever that their names were known beyond their own townships, or at most beyond their own counties, suddenly find that they are objects of interest in Boston, Philadelphia, Chicago, St. Louis, San Francisco, and yet more than in all the rest of the cities, in New York. Jones, who has not been making a very good year of it, and doubts whether, with the few hundreds of dollars remaining after his crops are sold, he can manage to squeeze through till the next spring, is suddenly electrified with the information contained in those pamphlets and circulars, that he can make money without work, and—yes, absolutely without risk. There cannot possibly be any doubt of the fact, for the circulars, especially, are as clear as—mud. They are full of explanations that explain nothing, and statements that can be made to state anything on occasion. All that can be made certain from them, to the ordinary mind, is one fact, and that one of the greatest consequence—that Jones has only to send on $10, or $20, or $50 to some firm of brokers in the City (say "Dorrance & Co.," for want of any better name), who will invest his money for him, at a charge so trifling that it really amounts to nothing,—watch the markets for him, buy and sell for him, and so manage the affair altogether that while he, the said Jones, is eating, sleeping, driving his horses on a pleasure excursion, or playing pool at the country tavern, his money will be doubling and quadrupling itself!

Would not Jones be a pretty sort of fool not to embrace so tempting an offer? He does embrace it, privately, so that no one else shall know how he is amassing wealth until the deed is accomplished. He tells no one—no one of these country speculators tells another, as a general rule; and the result is that no one, even if bitten and if brought to the knowledge that he is bitten, can and will do anything to warn others. Jones, and ten thousand other Joneses over the length and breadth of the land, fall into the trap, and they supply the villainous operators with the material on which to work, to the end of *getting a little money out of each, and thus amassing a great deal for themselves.*

Jones sends on the money just demanded by (we will say again) "Dorrance & Co." It goes without saying that "Dorrance & Co.," before soliciting his patronage, have laid some nice little plans by which his contributions, and the contributions of the twenty or fifty thousand others, can be made available to— somebody! And of course Jones, in the very act of accepting the suggestion of "Dorrance & Co." to invest at all, accepts their other suggestions of *how* he should invest, and authorizes them to buy "puts," "calls," "spreads," "straddles," or anything else that they may happen to recommend, with the "margin" understood and supplied. From that hour, Jones has entered the maelstrom. Let us see how he gets out of it!

XIV.

"MARGINAL OPERATIONS."

This phrase applies, as we have already seen, in some sense, to a very large proportion of transactions in stocks—no considerable proportion of them being paid for in full and at the time of purchase; but the same words may be especially applied to certain operations between the unscrupulous city broker and his customer in the country, whom he has deluded into "accepting his aid to make a fortune," through the pamphlets and circulars already named.

Suppose that Mr. Johnson, living at Peoria, sends on to Twistem, New York stock-broker, an order to buy him one hundred shares of Western Union, which he has been informed, by those circulars, is very likely to "boom" within a few days. Twistem buys the stock; but in charging for it, waits (see some previous transactions) until it has moved up and down once or twice, so that he can set it down at a proper figure (that is, proper and money-making for himself). So much for the purchase and the entry of it. Now for the sale of it, or some other things alternately connected. Suppose that Mr. Johnson wants the stock—to take it out of the hands of Twistem, and use it elsewhere. He cannot get it! No matter what amount of margin he may have put up on it, and no matter if he has been advised of the purchase, he cannot get it, if he remains in Peoria, because Twistem does not intend to let it go out of his own hands and so lose his opportunity of "handling" it. Sending for the stock, ten chances to one that he is told that the man from whom it was bought has not delivered it—that some small hitch is in the way, etc. Sending for the money after having ordered it sold, and been informed that it has been sold, he cannot get the money. The same story in another shape : the man who has made the purchase has suddenly proved to be very slow in making payment, though of course he will make it all right in a a few days, etc.

In a word, if Johnson has made a loss in the transaction, he is very certain to be informed of the fact at once, with the request for the necessary remittance and the assurance that "it will be all right next time;" and if he has happened to make a gain, *in spite of the fact of Twistem playing against him all the while*, he is no more likely to receive a settlement from Twistem, with the payment of balance by the latter, than he is to become King of the Friendly Islands. It may be said, in point of fact, that the purse of the broker is lined with fish-hooks and eel-spears. There is not much difficulty in the money going into it, because the barbs are all smooth in that direction; but, getting it out, all the points stick out with their full sharpness, and the thing won't come any how that they may try to fix it.

It must not be understood that the broker *never* pays the money due his customer. It is not "never," but "hardly ever," if we may be allowed to quote "Pinafore" in a grave and very serious financial article. When he does pay, however, one of two things is the case: he has been brought to book, through the presence of his customer or the services of a lawyer in his behalf; or he sees the chances of a bigger haul, settles with a good grace, and looks for the next and bigger profit out of the good character thus established.

One word more on this point. In any case in which the discretion of handling a margin has been left entirely in the hands of the broker, with full trust in him on the part of the customer, and no positive directions whatever—the question of eventually winning or losing is settled. He will probably have his hopes buoyed, now and again, by some account of a success, but that account of a success is always accompanied with notice that some other speculation employing his money has been entered upon, promising even better results. Generally, the new operation will require a little more money; and the customer, pleased with the success (!!) already won, forwards it. He may keep on doing so, until the day of doom; and things will remain very pleasant, except for his pocket-book or his bank-account. It is when he cries "enough!" and expresses his determination to have a settlement and deal no more, that he is at once "wiped out" by some terrible loss, which the broker could not have expected, which the whole financial world has been unable to foresee, which the broker regrets more than any one else can, etc., etc., etc.

XV.

Another Case at Length.

Suppose that Mr. Jenkinson, of Tideoute, Oil Districts, has authorized *his* favorite broker, Biteum, to purchase him a "call" on 100 shares of Erie. (The "call" has already been explained as *the right to demand* a certain amount of stock.) Biteum informs him that he has purchased the "call" at 45. He has not purchased it at all, in fact—made the contract himself, with intent to take all the advantages and nothing on the other side. When the "call" matures, the stock has advanced to 50 By any fair dealing, Jenkinson has made 5 per cent. on the shares, or $500, and Biteum has lost 5 per cent., or $500, less the commission. But does Biteum "own up?" Not much! To pay $500 out of his hard-earnings, would be very inconvenient, and indeed "something that we don't do, you know!" What can he do? What does he do? Of course he cannot hold Jenkinson off from any information, the latter writing to him every day or two. What does he do? Why he simply puts Jenkinson into a 60 days straddle on Okechobee and Hardpan for $600, bringing him $100 in debt.

Jenkinson, informed of his having made $500, and considering that the nest-egg of a fortune, is necessarily in a very good humor. While in this good humor, he receives from Biteum (who is also in a good humor, seeing that he is about to get out of his $500 loss so neatly, and make *his* nest-egg show up so capitally) the following pleasant epistle (in spirit the same, though in substance a trifle different, as one that may be found in "Dorrance & Co.'s" transactions, at near the commencement of this exposé):

Mr. JAMES JENKINSON,
Tideoute, Oil Districts.

MY DEAR SIR: I take great pleasure in notifying you that your call on 100 shares of Erie, maturing to-day, has been closed at 50, with net result (less $\frac{1}{16}$ for setting) of $493.75 to your advantage. I trust that the profit is satisfactory, and that as a compliment upon my efforts in your behalf, you will favor me with other and larger orders. I have taken the liberty (not having had time to communicate with you in the brief period allowed to decide on the movement) of placing your credit balance towards the purchase of a straddle on 100 shares of Okechobee and Hardpan, which stock, as I hear from the most reliable source (being myself closely interested in the clique now preparing for action), will show some very great changes within the next 60 days. There would seem to be no question of this privilege returning you from 300 to 500 per cent. profit on your outlay, at the very lowest calculation. You will please remit me the difference of account, $106.25, which gives you entire interest in the contract. As heretofore, I shall, if agreeable to you, use my very best endeavors in your behalf; and all that I desire or expect in return is a continuance of your favors, and a fitting publicity, among your friends and ac-

quaintances, to what success you may attain. It would, of course, be no disadvantage to yourself, if some of those friends and acquaintances should also become interested in a plan of stock operations at once so simple and so profitable. I remain, awaiting your favors, Very truly yours,
JOHN THADDEUS BITEUM.

Ten to one that Mr. Jenkinson falls into the trap, baited as it is with (apparent) previous success. He not only forwards the required $106.25, but acts upon the hint, so skillfully given him, to blow the horn of the broker. Some of the others tumble in; and Biteum's plan of at once killing off an old obligation and extracting more money is a splendid success. For it goes without saying that three or four times what has been reported made or due, is reported within a very few weeks lost on Okechobee and Hardpan; and thus the old, old story is told over again. [N. B.—This is a favorite plan, by the way, with the Biteums, when through carelessness or from any other cause they have not "tied up" the privilege before it has gained such profitable headway as to leave them in debt for several times the amounts at first extracted. How does it look before the public. and in the broad day-light of a few plain words?]

XVI.

Telegraphic Tricks.

Every one knows that the telegraph is one of the most powerful agencies of the earth, at the present day. Less than half a century has gone by since we knew nothing of it, and since the mails, here and there a semaphore telegraph (in which the wooden arms, thrown in various directions, conveyed information), and now and then a carrier-pigeon, carried all the intelligence that was not conveyed by the visit of one to another, in a carriage or on horseback if not on foot. To-day, every one all over the world can know everything that is occurring over any other part of it, or nearly so, with a certain expenditure of money for that advantage. Consequently, we are all more or less the slaves of the wires and of the little ticking affairs behind them, and some of us more truly so than were any of the Slaves of the Lamp or Slaves of the Ring of the old Aladdin days.

No one in the world uses the telegraph more, or to larger personal advantage, than the swindling so-called "broker," dealing with his customers at a distance. He well understands the somewhat startled feeling which we all experience in receiving a telegraphic message, compared with what we feel in the mere reception of a letter; and he plays accordingly upon the nerves of the person whom he desires financially to assault. He knows that Smith, Jones, and Robinson all feel the effect (as if the wire really ran through their own persons) when a dispatch is flashed to them—and that they say, in effect if not in words, "Good heavens! here *is* something of consequence! If it had not been, Gripem would have written me instead of telegraphing! Now I *must* act."

Gripem is in trouble. He has got himself in half a

dozen of the tangles alluded to in some of the late previous paragraphs, and nothing will save him from going to the dogs publicly (he has probably gone there privately long ago!) unless it is some so:t of *coup d`etat* quite as conclusive as that of Napoleon, even if on a more limited scale. He wires to one, two, ten or fifty of those customers who have not yet found him out to the extent of breaking with him, something like this :

JOHN SMITH, Gudgeonville, Ill.
Positive information concerning Bustup and Blueblazes. Large profits assured. Movement guaranteed. Remit all possible. Answer.
THEOPHILUS GRIPEM.

This is, taken all in all, a very neat operation. In the first place, the presumed costliness of telegraphing makes the receiver feel, as already said, that there must be "something in it," and at the same time it prevents his demanding or expecting that the dispatch should contain explicit information. And see how skillfully it is worded ! Not one phrase of absolute committal in the whole of it. "Movement guaranteed." Very likely; but was there any assurance given in what direction? "Large profits assured." Certainly—to somebody; but to whom? "Positive information;" that must go for what it is worth, always; it is so easy to say afterwards, "Well, I was only misinformed, that is all; and I made the very closest inquiries. How earnest I was in my belief is proved by the fact that I myself invested, and that I am nearly or quite ruined by the things going wrong." (The probabilities are, by the by, that there is not much difficulty in his proving *the latter part of the statement*, as he is nearly enough bankrupt to satisfy the most anxious inquiries).

Well, so much for the dispatch, and the calculations with which it has been manufactured. The effect has been already foreshadowed. Smith has a few hundreds lying idle, or a few hundreds that he can reach, in the hands of a friend, by giving a little due-bill and a small mortgage *that he can pay off so easily when he has made his money.* Everything looks right. The dispatch seems to be, and no doubt is, one in good faith. On such a basis nothing can well be lost, and everything may be gained by taking this *disinterested advice*, which gives him such an advantage. "Time is money," surely, now if never before. None of it must be lost. He has not time to make any investigation, and in point of fact he does not feel the necessity of any. He telegraphs, within an hour:

THEOPHILUS GRIPEM, New York:

Have remitted five hundred by mail, in reply to your telegram. Make all possible for me.

JOHN SMITH.

How do the two parties stand when this little operation has been concluded? Gripem has probably wired to twenty persons, in the same way—possibly to fifty, with slight changes in his phraseology. If twenty, ten of them have replied favorably. Result, $5,000 in hand—very much in hand, for it will never go out again, at least to the "contributors." If he has wired to fifty, he has probably twenty acceptances, and the still greater sum of $10,000. Guineas to pennies that not one of the whole array ever sees one dollar of the whole amount forwarded again, some one of the many tricks for covering up the villainy (a part of them already shown, and the rest very easily understood from them) being resorted to to hoodwink the destined victim and escape being shot down in the street (the latter especially if the "John Smith" is a man of a little farther west than Gudgeonville)!

At certain periods of stock excitement and fluctuation, when the fever seemed to extend over the whole land and the public were a body of idiots, the Western Union Telegraph Company have made thousands upon thousands of dollars in a single day, through the transmission of large lines of dispatches of the character of that lately given—every one a fraud (or if not every one, certainly ninety-nine hundredths of them) and all manufactured, without the least foundation, for the purpose of "bleeding by telegraph."

XVII.

Syndicates and Combinations.

A word, here, about one of the favorite allurements held out to those intended to be victimized—partially alluded to, already, in some portions of the preceding. This is the system of "combination"—sometimes called a "syndicate," and sometimes used under its plain name. When supposed fools are to be dealt with, the higher-sounding the name the better, as is evident to the meanest capacity; and so any body of men can pretty well estimate the regard in which they are held by those attempting to manage them, by noticing whether they are addressed in plain terms or favored with some of the largest words in the dictionary.

By what authority the favorite term, "syndicate," is used in any such combination, might be a puzzle if people were in the habit of looking for a reason in anything. A syndicate is nothing more nor less than a justice, or officer of justice, in any country where the word is known and means anything—except sometimes in France, where it signifies an assignee in bankruptcy. Perhaps, if that signification were known and admitted for it here, the general understanding would be the plainer. The United States government uses it for some of their foreign loan transactions; and so of course those who wish to be very "high up" use it in transactions much smaller. But all this really has nothing to do with the question whether any one of these "combinations" amounts to anything more than a means of creating confidence that has no foundation whatever.

Now it does amount to nothing, almost always— especially in stock-dealing. When it has any force, in the way of a great-named agreement made in some one of the cities, to carry out a certain end in the way of bolstering up one certain stock or pulling down another, it is very easy to understand that outsiders, and so-called brokers, of no personal or financial standing, are not admitted behind the curtain or allowed to have any share in the advantages, until the chance has gone by and there is really nothing more to be made out of it. Some hint may come into possession of the Gripems and Biteums, and they may display their supposed knowledge in flaming circulars and explanatory pamphlets, but they will be attempting a swindle all the same, and those who take any chances in them are almost certain to find that the axiom that "union is strength," merely means, in their case, *a union of several influences* to get money out of their pockets, while more than all the "syndicates" of the century would be necessary to get one dollar of it back again into them.

It may as well be said, here, once for all, that all offers of great opportunities sent out into the country are swindles, or if they are not swindles, blunders, which amount to very nearly the same thing. Against what are any of these "syndicates" or "combinations" intended to operate, at the best? Why, against great corporations and chartered combinations, having ten times as much money as could possibly be collected together by any one of these operators; and, as a consequence, even if any of these operators should chance to be honest and straight-forward (which does not seem very likely), they would be simply fools, going to ruin and leading there all who trusted them with their money.

Not one dollar should be forwarded, by any man, at the request of any circular, pamphlet, telegram, or any other general demand. Not one dollar should be advanced without full explanations of what is intended to be done, or without close knowledge on the part of the person making the advance, as to the character and standing of the person requesting it. If this system should be adopted there would be a rapid falling off, at once, in the number and importance of stock-dealing swindles.

XVIII.

KNOWING WHO MAKE AND TAKE THE CONTRACTS.

Here, too, is a thing of no secondary importance. Not one dollar in ten could be extracted from the pockets of customers, even if they dealt in stocks at all, if the demand was always made, and enforced, to know *who make the contracts ;* what reputable firm sold the privileges announced as having been purchased, and who was prepared to stand by them at the day of settlement. There *are* reputable and first-class dealers who make stock-contracts—such men and such firms as Russell Sage, James Keene, O. M. Bogert, H. Kennedy, Norbury & Co., and many others who could be named. When assurance is given that one of these has made a contract, it is likely to amount to something, and the customer may have some hope of being able to avail himself of the favorable changes of the markets.

But to send money to Squeezem, and have Squeez-

connection, and in that way possibly commanding more practical attention than as scattered through the preceding pages. By following these rules, or as nearly following them as may be practicable, intending dealers will escape many of the perils that surround careless and unforbidden plunges into everything promising excitement with the least hope of profit.

Rule First.—Don't attempt to make any investment whatever in stocks, except with money the loss of which would not be absolute ruin, and with money the being kept out of which for a considerable time would not seriously peril comfort or credit. Many a man has made himself miserable by a hasty investment, the trouble being that he began to worry over the need the moment the money was out of his hands. And many a man has destroyed what chances he may really have enjoyed for making money, by being so pressed that he could not leave the working powers to do the good that was really in it. Many a year ago, a well-known man about town used sometimes to "take a hand in" at games of chance; and when he did so, those who were in his company always knew him to take from his pocket-book a certain amount of money (more or less, according as he felt at the moment), put back the remainder, and say, as he commenced to put his stake on the board: "There—that is what I am going to allow myself to lose to-night; just that and no more." Very often, perhaps quite as often as the reverse, he did not lose it, or any part of it; it may have happened that very often he was a winner, at all events he escaped worrying over the results. Intending investors may take a hint from him, and if they do not keep out of the thing altogether, at least so operate that they do not involve themselves deeper and deeper, "sending good money after bad," as the gamblers sometimes say, and doing what their judgment would not have allowed them to do, simply because they have already done something imprudent.

Rule Second.—Don't pay any attention to flaming and attractive circulars and pamphlets. In ninety-nine cases out of one hundred, dealers who have anything really good, will find means of placing themselves and their "bonanzas" before the investing public, without any extra effort whatever. It does not *always* follow that what is speciously and flamingly announced is a swindle or blunder; but the chances lie in that direction, and at least the rule is a safe one to touch no edge of the "chance" thus offered, without diligent inquiry, and at least something more to recommend it than the mere assertion of the interested dealer, who generally has no objection to representing chalk as cheese, and pyrites of iron as ore filled with solid gold. The circulars thus sent may be found very useful for gun-wadding, for the lighting of fires, and for other domestic uses that need not be mentioned ; and the pamphlets (if the paper is not too heavy) may answer corresponding purposes. Far better put them to such uses than to pin any faith upon them and invest any good money on their promises, *without due and careful investigation.*

Rule Third.—Don't operate on margin with any

firm not members of some Exchange or Board of Brokers, or not represented in either of those bodies.

Rule Fourth.—Don't imagine that one per cent. is a margin sufficient to carry any operation successfully, or wonder if the small amount of money is lost that is so unwisely invested.

Rule Fifth.—Request references, always, from brokers whom you do not know, and examine those references before closing any important business with them. Better still, make the same request and the same examination before closing *any*.

Rule Sixth.—Never give an order leaving the discretion with the broker. Human nature is fallible, as are human pocket-books; and no man can tell the hour at which a man who actually intended to treat you fairly, may find the temptations too strong to be resisted, to become your enemy—that is, to have interests opposed to yours. Give your own order for purchases and sales, and see that it is carried out, or insist on knowing the reason why, and holding the person defaulting to account.

Rule Seventh.—Don't invest in capitalizations, combinations, syndicates, or pools, of any shape or character, unless with satisfactory vouchers from those with whom the contracts are made.

Rule Eighth.—Never send money by mail, unless registered, except in bank-checks, drafts, or money orders.

Rule Ninth.—When purchasing Stock Privileges, have all information with reference to the original contracts forwarded to you, in case the circumstances are such that the contract itself needs to be retained for use. [We have already named some of the responsible men for the securing of such contracts, but may repeat the names of Russell Sage, James R. Keene, O. M. Bogert, Harvey Kennedy, J. Braine, Norbury & Co., Musgrave & Co., J. G. Mills, Newcomb, and occasionally members of the Exchange.]

Rule Tenth.—Don't forget that no contracts are issued for less than 100 shares by any of the large dealers named, or by many others, and that though they may be secured for a less number, through small dealers, the highest authority is always the best and most reliable.

Rule Eleventh.—Don't expect any of the operations of Wall Street or its neighborhood to be entirely without risk (there would not be any money in them, if they were!); and don't consider that the world is coming to an end in the event of loss in an operation against which you have (now, at least) had due warning, and for the conducting of which all possible instructions have been honestly and fairly given.

XX.

SOME PARTICULARS OF THE NEW YORK STOCK EXCHANGE.

The title of this little book is "Fraud and Fair Dealing in Stocks." We have had so much to say, necessarily, of frauds, that the careless reader may come to the conclusion that there is nothing honest in the whole business, and nothing reliable lying behind it. It now becomes our duty, in closing, to show something very different, in an institution founded upon, and devoted entirely to, stocks, commanding the confidence of the whole financial world.

The New York Stock Exchange was founded in 1792. The following agreement, signed by the charter members and others subsequently admitted, was the basis of business until 1820:

We, the subscribers, brokers for the purchase and sale of Public Stocks, do hereby solemnly promise and pledge ourselves to each other, that we will not buy or sell from this day, for any person whatsoever, any kind of Public Stocks at a less rate than one quarter per cent. commission on the specie value, and that we will give a preference to each other in our negotiations. In testimony whereof, we have set our hands this 17th day of May, at New York, 1792.

Lem. Bleeker,
Hugh Smith,
Armstrong & Barnewall,
Samuel Marsh,
Bernard Hart,
Alexander Zunty,
Andrew D. Barclay,
Empn. Hart,
Julian McIvers,
G. N. Bleecker,
Peter Inspach,
David Reedy,

Sutton & Hardy,
Benjamin Seixas,
John Heary,
John A. Hardenbrook,
Amurt Beebee,
Benjamin Winthrop,
James Ferrers,
Isaac M. Goemez,
Augustine H. Lawrence,
John Besly,
Charles McIvers, Jr.,
Robinson & Hartshorn.

November 13, 1792.

Daily meetings and the regular call of stocks commenced in 1820. The sessions of the Board were held at various places—first, in a room in the neighborhood of Jauncey Court; then in the room of some broker; with occasional out-door meetings under a buttonwood tree on Wall Street, near Pearl. Finally, the Board established itself in the Merchants' Exchange, where it continued to hold it sessions until 1853. It then moved into a room in the Commercial Exchange Bank Building, where it remained until 1858. From 1858 until December, 1865, it occupied rooms in Lord's Building, with entrances on William and Beaver Streets. It then moved to its present quarters. The present Exchange Building, although commodious and well located, is far from meeting the requirements of the Board, and it is probable that a new building will, at no distant day, be erected.

A parchment book, containing the signatures of the members of the Stock Exchange from the date of organization, shows the autographs of Mr. Charles Marvin, one of the oldest and staunchest members now living; Mr. Charles Graham, also living at the present time; and many other prominent gentlemen who are still connected with the Exchange, among whom we noticed the name of Mr. Henry G. Stedman, the oldest and one of the most esteemed members living, who has just been made President of the

Rapid Transit Committee. Mr. Stedman is widely noted for his brilliant oratorical powers and remarkable talents as a public speaker.

XXI.

Consolidation of the Boards.

The three boards—the New York Stock Exchange, the Open Board of Brokers, and the United States Government Board, were consolidated in May, 1869. The first president elected was Mr. William Nelson; next in successive order were Messrs. William Seymour, Jr., William B. Clarke, Edward King (who is now President of the Union Trust Company), Henry G. Chapman, George M. Broadhead, George W. McClean, Salem T. Russell, Henry Meigs, and lastly Brayton Ives, now presiding. These gentlemen were elected in the month of May of each consecutive year, in the order in which they are mentioned.

No president has ever been re-elected, each having served for a single term of one year; a new departure will be made this year, however, in the nomination of Mr. Brayton Ives, the present incumbent, for a second term.

During the war, the Stock Exchange, for the purpose of sustaining the Government, passed a resolution prohibiting members from selling Government Bonds "short," and another forbidding all dealings in gold. The passage of these resolutions cost the members of the Exchange millions of dollars, but was of incalculable value to the Government. It was through this action of the Stock Exchange that the formation of the Gold Exchange was brought about.

The New York Stock Exchange is one of the most important financial organizations in the world. It may be likened to the great balance wheel, governing and regulating a gigantic power which moves all the intricate machinery of capital in this country, and largely affects all the monetary interests of great foreign centres of trade. Its membership comprises a class of men in whom immense wealth, extraordinary enterprise, unusual alertness, and exceptional abilities, are respectively leading characteristics. The operations are of mighty import, the transactions leap to and fro instantaneously, and almost lightning calculations must flash through the brain to meet emergencies. At any hour, the even tenor of the always stirring events may be changed to a whirlwind of excitement. A crisis in certain stocks is a periodical occurrence, and panics may rage at almost any season. Men who pass their days and lives in this atmosphere, have a constant tension and nerve and sudden shocks of mental excitement that can only be appreciated by realization; description of the strain on vitality is simply impossible. It seems like a rapid transit to death. But on an average they are healthy men, because their nerves, minds, and bodies are trained to it, and fortified for its emergencies.

XXII.

A WEALTHY ONE THOUSAND.

To-day the New York Stock Exchange has a membership of over one thousand, and for wealth it exceeds all other stock organizations in the world. The daily deposits and credits of brokers in city banks and trust companies, are estimated in hundreds of millions, and the par value of annual sales made at the boards and "over the counter" is computed as considerably exceeding $22,000,000,000.

The Government and the Open Boards were consolidated with the old historic Stock Exchange in May, 1869, and its organic law is marked by a conservatism that imparts character and strength to the Association, as its high representative position demands.

The office of the President is mainly executive, and there is a Treasurer of semi-annual importance; there is one Vice-President, a Secretary with his assistants, and the Roll Keeper, severally intrusted with the duties appertaining to similar officers in every organization, and with the special and extremely arduous work incident to the daily sessions. The real executive control, however, now rests with a Governing Committee, consisting of forty members selected from the whole body, together with the President and Treasurer, in their unofficial capacity. All duties of administration, of legislation, devolve on this committee, which is divided into four classes, one of which goes out each year; and the committee, like its associate officers, is subject in a certain degree to the will of its constituency. But beyond its right of election at the annual meeting, the Board is nearly powerless.

The Governing Committee may make or unmake, suspend, expel, or re-admit. It may even alter the entire letter of the constitution or by-laws, and unless two-thirds of all the members of the Association disapprove thereof within one week, the changes become final law. So full an attendance of this Board as is required by this rule is almost unexampled, and the committee is therefore practically as autocratic as the Venetian Council of Ten.

This Governing Committee, in reference to its varied functions, consists of seven sub-divisions, whose duties correspond to the distinct objects for which the Association was created. The most vital of these objects are:

First. The rigid scrutiny of all securities liable to be dealt in by the Exchange.

Second. A proper surveillance over members in respect to their fidelity to contracts, and a stringent examination of the good character and responsibility of candidates for membership.

Third. A systematization of brokerage, so far as it relates to the intercourse of member with member.

No stock, bond or other security can be dealt in by the Board, unless all the financial conditions, capital, number of shares, resources, etc., have been searchingly examined. As an additional safeguard, the Exchange binds itself to exclude any active speculative stock of any company which fails to keep a registry of shares in some responsible trust company, bank, or similar agency, and to give due public notice of any intention to increase its capital, either through the conversion of bonds, or by direct issue, with the grounds of such increase.

XXIII.

The Admission of Members.

The rules for the admission of members, and for the government of those already enrolled in the organization, are necessarily very strict. In an arena where a mere nod may seal a contract involving hundreds of thousands of dollars, and a whisper is as binding as the longest and most cunningly phrased agreement of all the lawyers, men must have keen intellects, vast experience, and spotless business reputations. Every debt, as well as every offer made and accepted, must be rigidly fulfilled. A member who fails must notify the President at once; he, in turn, promptly announces it to the Board; the Secretary records the name on the fatal list; the stock which has occasioned the default is sold, or bought, in open market *under the rule;* and the broker loses every privilege of the Exchange until his creditors are satisfied, and the Governing Committee consents to his reinstatement.

The Exchange has guarded itself against the hazards of failure, compelling "weak" members to supplement their contracts by a heavy money deposit, punishing fraud by expulsion, rendering suspension a severe penalty by its network of rules framed out of extreme solicitude for the rights of the creditor. Not less exacting are the provisions for new membership. Brokers' clerks—representing that alert, quick-witted, agile class which has grown up under the rough tuition of the street, knows its laws, comprehends the abiding sacredness of its verbal contracts—find the doors of admission open much more readily than do men whose experience is limited to two or three years as capitalists, brokers, or bankers. The latter indeed must show a very clean record, and sub mit to a scrutiny in its very nature extremely irksome.

In former years the black-ball played an efficient part in winnowing out candidates; and the new regimen, although probably free from the influences of personal dislike, is likely in other ways to be not less exacting.

That portion of the government which concerns itself with the terms of each several class of contracts and the regular order of busines, is a curious blending of law and usage; the latter being as strictly enforced as the former, although finding no place in the by-laws.

One point, however, is worthy of particular consideration. In all the great European share-marts, there is a general executive organization differing only in local details from that by which the New York Exchange is regulated. But the functions of the officers cease at the moment when the real business of a stock market begins. The syndic of the

Paris Bourse, it is true, presides over the daily sessions; but his duties are wholly subordinate, and the *agens de change* in the Corbeille—that basket-like chamber where the *parquet* assembles—direct the market quite at their pleasure. In the London Stock Exchange even this semblance of authority is wanting. The daily meetings are simply the confluence of a mob, in which everybody bargains with everybody, where there is no order, no system, and no record of transactions.

XXIV.

Completeness and Business.

The New York Stock Exchange in this regard has a completeness to be found in no similar transatlantic organization. The securities dealt in by the Board are divided into two classes, known respectively as the Regular and the Free List. No bond or stock has been, or can be enrolled, in either of these classes, without due scrutiny in committee ; and the ground of separation is simple. The regular list must be called in sequence by the Chairman in the chair ; the free list may, or may not be called, at the option of members ; of course the former is the important class, and includes nearly three hundred distinct securities, comprising all the great railway shares and bonds, State and City securities, bank stock, and a curious *melange* of express, telegraph, mining shares, etc., enumerated as "miscellaneous."

At half-past ten o'clock in the morning, daily, the Chairman ascends the rostrum in the official chamber of the Stock Exchange, and goes through the selected list thus: Miscellaneous stocks; railroad stocks; State bonds; City stocks; railroad bonds. The assembled brokers, with their budget of orders, wait expectant, and the instant a stock is reached that is in their day's book, they spring into the arena with their bid or offer. When a "speculative" or favorite stock is called, the excitement heightens, and the air is rent with their rival shouts. The presiding officer repeats the transactions to the Assistant Secretary at his side, who promptly records them, while the "maker," or blackboard clerk, writes off the prices upon the table at the head of the room. Where there is a doubt regarding buyer or seller, the Chairman decides, subject to immediate appeal in case of dissatisfaction, such brokers only as witnessed the transaction voting.

As soon as the regular call is completed, the free list is in order, and the Chairman repeats the name of such stocks as the members may select for dealings, the Assistant Secretary recording every bid, and accompanying details. After this the session closes, unless the members in attendance wish to call up anew particular stocks on the regular list; this provision allows of dealings in those securities which were hastily passed over in the routine morning call.

At one o'clock the afternoon session is held, over which the second Vice-Chairman usually presides. The usages of the morning board prevail here as well. The Vice-Chairman holds the market in his hands, directs all movements, announces each transaction, and arbitrates all disputes. The Assistant Secretary also renews his record of all bidding, and in his book at the close the whole history of the day appears.

Fifteen minutes before the first meeting of the Regular Board, the Government Board begins its sessions in an adjoining chamber. The same routine is observed: a Vice-Chairman directs the market; an Assistant Secretary notes down against each class of national securities, as it passes the gauntlet of the brokers, the prices offered and demanded, and every important feature of a transaction, in case of positive sale. Were the stock dealings of Wall Street limited to these two rooms, an efficient safeguard would exist against some of the most perilous phases of speculation. But it has happened, partly on account of the great volume of daily business, that members may bargain with members for the sale and purchase of active stocks through the day, and which is continually done by groups around the room or main hall.

Next in usefulness, of the officers, is the Roll Keeper, who records the fines; and no body of men, to all appearance, are more fond of breaking over all minor rules and promptly meeting the penalty than New York stockbrokers. The annual dues of the Exchange are only fifty dollars, but the fines of individual members sometimes aggregate to nearly ten times that sum. Any interruption to the presiding officer, while calling stocks, renders a broker liable to a penalty of "not less than twenty-five cents" for each offence. To smoke a cigar within the Exchange costs five dollars. The same fine, or less, at the discretion of the President, is imposed for nonattendance at special meetings. A broker cannot stand on a table or chair without paying a fine of a dollar, and if he innocently flings a "paper dart" at a neighbor, he is fined ten dollars, and all the way from one to five dollars to do anything, not enumerated in these offences, which may be judged indecorous by the presiding officer. Thus it will be seen that the business of stock brokerage—that is, all the business as regulated by the stringent rules of the Stock Exchange, is absolutely surrounded by the most complete protection against irresponsibility, and, as far as any legitimate avocation can be, is rendered unquestionably honorable, legitimate, and thoroughly reliable.

XXV.

IN CONCLUSION,

We are pleased to be able to set down the last word of the previous paragraph, in taking leave of the subject which it has been our duty to handle briefly, but with plain expressions, and for the good of the community. Most previous articles on the subject of which we have spoken, have had some motive behind them, rendering their statements often doubtful in important particulars: we think that we may fairly claim exemption from any such charge, in giving "Fraud and Fair Dealing in Stocks" to the public.

www.ingramcontent.com/pod-product-compliance
Lightning Source LLC
Chambersburg PA
CBHW020258090426
42735CB00009B/1133